Meet a Baby Crocodile

Jon M. Fishman

D1518350

Lerner Publications ◆ Minneapolis

Lerner Publications Company
A division of Lerner Publishing Group, Inc.
241 First Avenue North
Minneapolis, MN 55401 USA

For reading levels and more information, look up this title at www.lernerbooks.com.

Library of Congress Cataloging-in-Publication Data
Names: Fishman, Jon M., author.
Title: Meet a baby crocodile / Jon M. Fishman.
Description: Minneapolis : Lerner Publications, 2017. | Series: Lightning bolt books. Baby Australian animals | Includes bibliographical references and index. | Audience: Ages 6 to 9. | Audience: Grades K to 3.
Identifiers: LCCN 2016043827 (print) | LCCN 2016054726 (ebook) | ISBN 9781512433906 (lb : alk. paper) | ISBN 9781512455878 (pb : alk. paper) | ISBN 9781512450545 (eb pdf)
Subjects: LCSH: Crocodiles—Infancy—Australia—Juvenile literature.
Classification: LCC QL666.C925 F57 2017 (print) | LCC QL666.C925 (ebook) | DDC 597.98/21392—dc23

LC record available at https://lccn.loc.gov/2016043827

Manufactured in the United States of America
1-42026-23896-12/2/2016

Table of Contents

From Egg to Baby

A mother Australian saltwater crocodile scrapes the ground. She makes a nest. She lays about fifty eggs in the nest.

Crocodiles build nests near water. Floods sometimes cover crocodile nests in water. The nests help protect the eggs from floods.

Crocodile nests are made of plants and mud.

The mother crocodile guards the nest. She keeps her eggs safe from predators.

If a mother crocodile does not protect her nest, lizards or pigs might eat her eggs.

The eggs start to hatch in about ninety days. Once the baby crocodiles are hatched, they are called hatchlings. They are about 11 inches (28 centimeters) long. That's as long as a sheet of notebook paper.

Emptying the Nest

The mother crocodile listens for sounds from her nest. *Chirp! Chirp!* The hatchlings call to their mother. She digs up the nest to uncover the hatchlings.

Sometimes a baby crocodile can get out of its egg without help.

If a baby has trouble getting out of its egg, the mother will help. The mother crocodile gently rolls the egg in her mouth to break the shell. This helps the baby hatch.

The mother picks up each hatchling in her mouth. She carries it to the water.

This hatchling sits on its mother. It is resting in the water.

The mother stays with the hatchlings. She protects them from predators such as adult crocodiles.

Crocodile hatchlings look like small adult crocodiles.

Learning to Hunt

Crocodile eggs have yolks. The yolks feed the babies before they hatch. After they hatch, the hatchlings eat the rest of the yolk.

An egg yolk can feed a hatchling for up to two weeks.

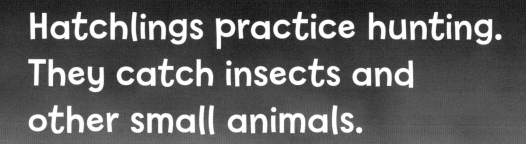

Hatchlings practice hunting. They catch insects and other small animals.

Hatchlings catch insects in their strong jaws. Adult crocodiles have the strongest bites in the world.

The hatchlings grow. They begin to hunt bigger prey. They eat fish, birds, snakes, and small mammals.

Crocodiles hunt mostly at night. They wait in the water for prey to come near. They sneak up on prey from underwater.

Crocodiles are hard to spot in the water. Only their eyes poke above the surface.

Growing Up

The young crocodiles leave their mother after about eight months. They spend most of their time alone.

Crocodiles are cold-blooded. They lie in the sun to warm up. When they get too hot, they go into the water to cool off.

This crocodile is warming up in the sun.

A female crocodile is ready to lay eggs when she is ten to twelve years old. A male is ready for a mate at about sixteen years of age.

A full-grown male crocodile (*left*) is bigger than a full-grown female crocodile (*right*).

Most crocodiles live for forty to seventy years. Some may live as long as one hundred years!

Crocodile Life Cycle

Time until eggs hatch:
ninety days

Baby crocodile eats yolk and prey right away

Fully grown:
ten to sixteen years

Life span:
forty to
one hundred years

Leaves
its mother:
eight months

Habitat in Focus

- Saltwater crocodiles don't just live in Australia. They swim long distances to Asia and islands in the Pacific Ocean.

- People need to be careful when they are in a crocodile habitat. Crocodiles attack and kill people every year. But people are far more dangerous to crocodiles than crocodiles are to people.

- The temperature of the nest determines whether baby crocodiles will be male or female. More males hatch when the nest is warm. Females hatch when the nest is cooler.

Fun Facts

- Crocodiles speak to one another. They make at least four different noises!

- Saltwater crocodiles are the largest reptiles in the world.

- Crocodiles don't chew their food. They swallow stones to help break up food in their stomach.

- Crocodiles have been around for a long time. They come from a group of animals that is more than 205 million years old.

Glossary

cold-blooded: having a body temperature that changes depending on the temperature outside

flood: a large amount of water covering land

hatchling: a baby crocodile

mammal: an animal that gives milk to its young and usually has hair

mate: a partner

predator: an animal that hunts other animals for food

prey: animals that other animals eat

yolk: the yellow part of an egg that provides food for the baby

Further Reading

Active Wild: Saltwater
Crocodile Facts for Kids
http://www.activewild.com/saltwater
-crocodile-facts-for-kids

Australia Zoo: Reptiles—Saltwater Crocodile
https://www.australiazoo.com.au/our-animals
/reptiles/crocodilians/saltwater-crocodile

Discovery Kids: Australia Zoo
http://discoverykids.com/games/australia-zoo

Marsico, Katie. *Saltwater Crocodiles*. New York:
Children's Press, 2014.

Owings, Lisa. *Learning about Australia*.
Minneapolis: Lerner Publications, 2016.

Silverman, Buffy. *Can You Tell an Alligator from a
Crocodile?* Minneapolis: Lerner Publications, 2012.

Index

Photo Acknowledgments

The images in this book are used with the permission of: © Sergey Uryadnikov/Shutterstock.com, p. 2; © ANT Photo Library/Science Source, pp. 4, 19 (crocodile eating fish); © Tom Boyden/Lonely Planet Images/Getty Images, p. 5; © Auscape/Universal Images Group/Getty Images, pp. 6, 11; © Jurgen Freund/Minden Pictures, p. 7; © Graham Anderson/Science Source, p. 8; © Mike Parry/Minden Pictures, pp. 9, 16; © Michael Pitts/naturepl.com, p. 10; © Anadolu Agency/Getty Images, p. 12; © tbkmedia.de/Alamy, p. 13; © David Curl/npl/Minden Pictures, p. 14; © dirkr/Shutterstock.com, p. 15; © Konrad Wothe/NPL/Minden Pictures, p. 17; © Jeffrey W. Lang/Science Source, p. 18; © Juniors Bildarchiv GmbH/Alamy, p. 19 (eggs); © Meister Photos/Shutterstock.com, p. 19 (crocodile alone); © Dmitry Mozhzherin/Shutterstock.com, p. 22.

Front cover: © Anadolu Agency/Getty Images.

Main body text set in Billy Infant regular 28/36. Typeface provided by SparkType.